Dear Mrs Coop[...],

I wrote this over self healing myself and with a new mindset, healing grown a lot and finally becoming a version of myself that I always knew I could be. This is a collection of words that I wish someone had said to me during uncertain times and a few of these things were said to me in a myriad of ways by you. Thank you for the impact you have had in my life.

Warm Wishes,

Simra

10/11/2022

First Edition 2022

Published by Mad Pencil Publications
@the.madpencilpublications

© Copyright Protected by the author

All rights reserved. No part of the material protected by this copyright may be reproduced or utilized in any form, electronic or mechanical, including photocopying, recording, or by any information storage and retrieval system, without prior written permission from the copyright owner.

Follow me on

@syrwritings
@simrayasmin

@syrwritings

A Daily Reminder

By Simra Yasmin Rana

Dear Reader,

This is from Me to You

Have you stopped today to give thanks and have gratitude for this moment in your life? Go ahead, do it now and write 3 things you are grateful for below

-

-

-

Feeling better? Lighter even? That is the effect having gratitude does for you. Try doing this every day and see how much clearer and calmer your mindset will become.

You don't know enough to worry, just remember that worrying is betting against yourself and betting against yourself is wasted energy

You haven't even realised how you have lit up rooms and inspired people just by being you. Your energy is magnetic, and you don't even realise it. Start recognising all you are worth and all you have to offer this world.

the way they saw you was not specifically designed for you, as you are different and different can be scary to people who never had the courage to be their own self.

There are moments in life where you must remind yourself that you're something special. That you can't be replaced… where your mind, your heart, your conversation and your care, can't be replaced. By anyone.

Something beautiful will happen for you today, if you allow yourself to see the world through a new lens

Growth requires us to leave something behind, whether it's old habits, past beliefs, a mindset that you have outgrown and sometimes, even people. Allowing yourself to feel the losses in the midst of growth is vital as you will mourn your former life to make room for a new one

There's no competition when you are manifesting your own life. Every decision, every thought and every action are your own. It's up to you whether they are constructive or destructive

An affirmation for you:

I am allowing myself to rest without any guilt. I am giving myself time to recover and mentally recharge. I am in the process of creating a life for myself that feels balanced and true to me. I am creating my own reality. I am taking charge of the direction of my life.

Can I tell you something? – nothing that is meant for you will pass you by. Let beautiful connections pass through without attachment. Let yourself put your heart into the places and people that ignite something deep into your soul. If you do that, I promise you that the right things will stay. You will never truly lose what is for you.

Be connected to everything without being attached to anything.

It is not your duty to make your truth make sense to someone else.
Let your truth be known and everything else will fall into place naturally

Hope is with you. It's always been in front of you and it's never as far as it may seem.

Breath by breath. That is how you get through.

Don't be afraid to let go because there is nothing lonelier than losing yourself trying to please people that were never meant for you.

There will be only so many weekends you can live for,
summers you can long for,
winters you can let pass by before all you are doing is idly floating through life.
Take today and every day after to stop and love all that you are and all that is.

Here is just a reminder to be kind to yourself today

What is meant to be revealed to you will be revealed to you at the right time

Before you try to make sense of things,
may you learn to make peace with things

If you happen to accomplish something today that you are proud of regardless of the weight it holds, it is significant. Allow yourself to celebrate it whilst also knowing that if you didn't accomplish that goal yet, it would not have made you any less of a person. Your worth is not attached to your accomplishments.

You can still know peace, joy and love, even when you feel like you haven't done enough.

Failure is measured by how you value success.

Pace yourself with each season,
 as you will learn to trust the timing of your life and your decisions.

Sometimes it's good to change perspective on what really matters most to you. When you go back to the fundamentals of it all, what truly makes you feel most yourself?

If you spend your life consistently chasing someone else's approval,
you are forgetting yourself in the process.
Approve of yourself fully and that is the only validation you will ever need.

Be with someone who makes you feel safe, who makes you feel appreciated. Their name instantly brings you comfort and joy. The sound of their voice is what makes you feel at home and their energy feels pure. Where their presence alone inspires you and motivates you to be better, not for them but for yourself. They are yours undoubtedly without being attached or needing but the intentions remain wanting. You want to be with them, you want to make a life with them. Be with someone who makes loving feel as easy as breathing.

Things happen unexpectedly and it can turn out to be everything you've ever needed. Without realising, what you may have wanted becomes mute, whilst what you truly need falls into your life, your heart and your mind.

Open your heart sincerely and eventually, one day you will find yourself leading the life you once could only dream of having.
This will require some changes,
but change is necessary for moving out of your comfort zone,
moving out of your comfort zone is necessary for growth and growth is necessary for creating a life that is right for you.
Through changes we grow.

If you live and think as if you are already where you want to be, you will get there so much faster just by rewiring your mind to live in a state of knowing and assurance that you are mentally already there. The physical will follow if you continue to work at the same pace your mind is.

There is so much love you can find within yourself before you find it elsewhere

Choosing to love without fear is courage

The only thing truly stopping you is yourself.

Break that mental barrier and see just how much you are capable of.

You never meet someone by chance. People walk in and out of your life as you and they choose for a reason, whether it teaches you a lesson or becomes an experience that shapes into a pinnacle for your life. Regardless of the outcome, there is a purpose for the meaningless and meaningful connections.

Don't chase money, chase passion.

Passion will lead to money, fulfilment and happiness.

Chasing money without passion will lead to an emptiness that will one day consume you.

Your passions are your purpose.

when you continuously show up for yourself and be present in day-to-day goals, you are enhancing your life in ways that your future self will be grateful for

Inner faith is the origin of success

It's okay to be frightened as long as you stay inspired

A little self-love mixed with a little confidence goes a long way

The fabric of society only means something if you allow it to.
Live without limitations

Don't hold back because in the end,
we only regret the chances we didn't take

A broken heart will also fix a broken vision. Sometimes pain is what is needed to find what is truly meant for you

Freedom is realising you have the power to control your own life

Increased comfortability equals increased vulnerability

You are worth more than being someone's 'maybe'
Choose someone who chooses you

Make sure to not let your life amount to just a collection of possessions,
 but allow it to amount to a collection of experiences.
Experiences are what will add to your life to make it whole

You were born for this moment,
to seize your opportunities and have no regrets moving forward.
For you are a force to be reckoned with in this life and the next

The song of nature,
 though we can't hear it,
it never ends

Each day is a new opportunity for a fresh path to begin and to leave behind old patterns

If you revolve your life around your problems,
that's all you will come to find.
So instead,
 focus on revolving your life around fulfilling your desires

Surround yourself with people who motivate you to move forward,
and who fill your heart with light,
as it will walk with you through the darkest of nights

In the midst of difficulty lies an opportunity

Set your standards high and keep them there,
Never lower them for anyone regardless of the situation.

Know your worth

Stop being so hard on yourself,
the best days of the rest of your life are still pending

Privacy is power,
No one can hurt you with knowledge they don't know

Take this moment to compliment yourself, whether it is based on your appearance or an aspect of your life you are proud of. The positive energy you put into yourself will reflect into your life

Push through because realise that you are young, and life goes on.
We spend so much time controlling the future, but the future doesn't exist.
Live for now.
Build your life in the now and stop waiting for tomorrow or the day after.
The only real thing we have is the present

Match the energy of the version of you that you want to be

Listen to your intuition,
it knows more than you,
it feels for you,
and it will guide you

If you could see yourself the way others see you,
You would be pretty proud of yourself

You are free to choose the way you react to any situation.
Don't let your emotions control you,
You control them.

Be compassionate towards yourself today.
You deserve to appreciate yourself,
You deserve to be kind to yourself,
Most importantly,
You deserve to recognise the progress you have made.

You will never make a difference by being like everyone else

It gets worse before it gets better,
trust me on that.
Healing isn't linear,
It's messy and unpredictable but,
You must heal in order to be able to truly move forward

Find someone who makes you feel secure enough to allow yourself to let your insecurities not only show but shine through,

 so that they may become the things that make you a more confident version of you. The right person will make this process of self-love so much easier to process,

  as they will have already loved those things you dislike about yourself.

To them, your insecurities are what make you glow

Your lover should be your equal,
Your confidant,
Your peace,
Your home,
Your safety,
Your comfortability,
Your pride and your laughter but,
You are responsible for your own happiness along with your independence,
 before anyone else can add to it

Finding your 'why' and finding a centre of gravity is a combination that will help to fulfil your deepest,

wildest and most daring desires.

As being a hundred percent sure of yourself whilst your passion for life has a deep and clear purpose,

 Finding this will shape you into a person whose decisions cannot be questioned

As long as you are happy in the career path you have chosen,
No one can tell you that you are unsuccessful
``

Everyday choose to consciously have your choices reflect your goals and aspirations, not your fears or hesitations

Life becomes easier when you begin to stop taking peoples words so personally, As you will come to realise that they are usually projecting an insecurity of their own

You deserve happiness,
You deserve healing,
You deserve grace,
You deserve comfort,
You deserve security,
You deserve good things and
You deserve to love yourself

You didn't go through all of that to now stop and make nothing of it.
Better days are ahead,
I promise.

Energy is emotionally expensive,
be mindful of who you give it to

You don't have to be the go-to person for people you can't go to

Let people show up for you in ways that are natural to them,
Then decide if that is enough for you.
Allow people to show you who they truly are

You don't have to do it all at once,
Take one step at a time and watch it make all the difference

Today's advice:

Make some coffee or matcha and write down what truly makes you feel most alive

Don't go back to less just because you are too impatient to wait for something better

Because ....

The best things in life are worth waiting for

Trust this chapter of your life,
You are the author of your story,
Create something beautiful with it

Celebrate not only who you have become, but who you fought not to turn into

There is a past version of yourself that is cheering you on,
Be proud of yourself and how far you have come

You will never be too much for someone who can't get enough of you

Space to be your own person,
Mutual Trust,
Calm Communication,
Respect of each other's opinions,
and
Selfless Listening,
are what will make your relationship easier

One day you will find someone who looks at you the same way you look at the things that brings you pure joy

You are not responsible for the negative reactions to your boundaries

You are capable of anything that you put your mind to.
It is just about whether you have the patience to execute it

Meetings do not occur by coincidence.
Nothings happens by accident.
The universe meant for you to meet.

An Affirmation for today:

I will give myself the love and the patience that I give to others

Have faith and trust in your natural wisdom

Let yourself be loved.

You are worthy of feeling that warmth and appreciation that you so often make others feel.

Spending time alone is the best thing you can do for yourself.
Allow yourself to mentally and emotionally heal.

Don't forget to stop and look at your surroundings today,
No matter what is happening in your life,
You can always find beauty in the little things

An affirmation for today:

Gratitude fills my life with more wealth than I could have ever imagined

Pay attention to your energy around different people,
Some give,
Others take

Refrain from telling yourself no,

When your heart says otherwise.

Let yourself move towards where you want to be

You are allowed to say no to the things that you don't want in your life

The universe will align the moments in your life once you make a decision

during the course of your life,
there will be changes that you like,
there will be changes that you dislike,
you will constantly be moving through these changes,
but if you decide to stand still,
you will stay stuck in the same place,
nothing will change,
until you decide to move again

some advice:

every so often,
get out of bed earlier,
before anyone else has woken up,
watch the sunrise and have gratitude for that moment,
feel the warmth of the morning sun,
soak it all in,
appreciate the serenity of what the world has to offer,
before it begins

You won't always make the right decision, Especially if you don't know what the right decision is.

What matters is how you choose to learn from the decisions you have made

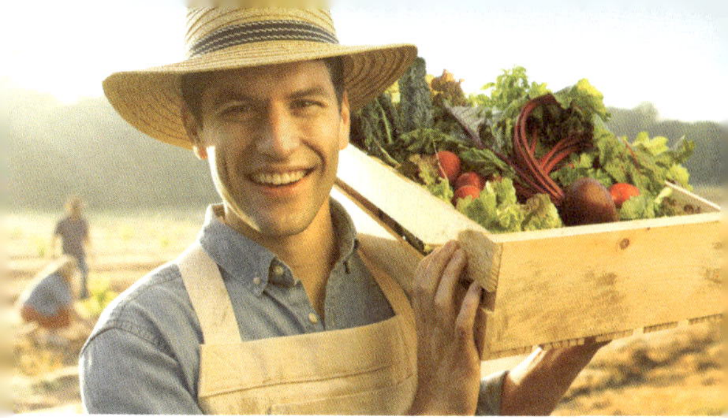

How will God's Kingdom solve our problems?

"The wicked will be no more . . .
The meek will possess the earth."
—*Psalm 37:10, 11.*

JW.ORG®

The Bible reveals that God's Kingdom

- Is a real government in heaven. —*Daniel 2:44; 7:14.*

- Will satisfy all of our needs. —*Isaiah 65:21-23.*

To learn more, go to jw.org.

© 2025 Watch Tower Bible and Tract Society of Pennsylvania

Druck: Wachtturm, Selters/Ts. Printed in Germany

When you can genuinely enjoy your own company and you get that feeling of being at peace with yourself,
Is when you know you can be your own version of home before anyone else

What does love feel like?

When you give it a shot without hesitation and your heart feels calm. You feel safe and you know you are loved. You are a team whilst holding their hand when they need it. They keep your heart soft through the harshness of what life can throw at you. Even when it can all feel overwhelming, they are a source of stability. Your journey together never feels boring, but it is exciting. You know it is right through every ounce of your body. Challenges you may face are worth it because you know they are worth the time. When you find someone who aligns effortlessly into your life, that is someone who deserves to know how special they are to you. Seldom does a connection like this form, maybe even once in a lifetime. Meeting someone who makes you breathe a bit deeper. Someone who you tell everything you desire to. Someone who you show the parts of yourself that you only ever thought you would see. Unconditional devotion. This is what love feels like.

Relationships require work but they should never feel like more energy than it's worth. Your partner is your equal, but you have different roles that should be equally matched.

Your needs are just as important as theirs. What you want matters just the same.

Asking for help does not make you weaker, It makes you stronger.

Being wise enough to know when you need a hand shows a level of maturity that most are too proud to ask for

You are more capable than you allow yourself to believe.

Have courage and be kind to yourself so you can project that positivity onto your goals.

You will have no limits to what you can achieve if you prioritise it is what you want.

This is a reminder to reaffirm any doubts you had or may have in the future. Come back to this moment, to any page and remember who you are, remember what you want and remember what you deserve.

Yours Sincerely,

S.Y.R.

Simra Y Rana writes to inspire and empower any one who reads her work, whether you're eight or eighty, Simra's words are written for you.

She started putting down her thoughts on paper from a young age, through growing up in Hertfordshire, England and Cambridgeshire, England, into adolescence she realised her words could help and relate to her readers. Growing up in an environment where writing was her escape, she aims to enlighten and motivate her readers as if she was talking to them herself. Whilst being an entrepreneur who has her own company, being a writer has always been her passion. You never feel alone whilst reading her work because you never are.

You can connect with Simra Y Rana on

@syrwritings
@simrayasmin  @syrwritings

to get your daily dose of positivity and healthy reminders.

Printed in Great Britain
by Amazon